# The Wiersbe
## BIBLE STUDY SERIES

I CORINTHIANS

The

# Wiersbe
## BIBLE STUDY SERIES

Discern the

Difference

between

Man's Knowledge

and

God's Wisdom

David C Cook
*transforming lives together*

THE WIERSBE BIBLE STUDY SERIES: 1 CORINTHIANS
Published by David C Cook
4050 Lee Vance View
Colorado Springs, CO 80918 U.S.A.

David C Cook Distribution Canada
55 Woodslee Avenue, Paris, Ontario, Canada N3L 3E5

David C Cook U.K., Kingsway Communications
Eastbourne, East Sussex BN23 6NT, England

The graphic circle C logo is a registered trademark of David C Cook.

All Scripture quotations in this study are taken from the Holy Bible, New
International Version®, NIV®. Copyright © 1973, 1978, 1984 by Biblica, Inc.™ Used
by permission of Zondervan. All rights reserved worldwide. www.zondervan.com.

In the *Be Wise* excerpts, unless otherwise noted, all Scripture quotations are taken
from the King James Version of the Bible. (Public Domain.) Scripture quotations
marked NIV are taken from the Holy Bible, New International Version®, NIV®.

All excerpts taken from *Be Wise*, second edition, published by David C Cook
in 2010 © 1982 Warren W. Wiersbe, ISBN 978-1-4347-6636-6.

ISBN 978-1-4347-0376-7
eISBN 978-1-4347-0491-7

The Team: Steve Parolini, Karen Lee-Thorp, Amy Konyndyk,
Sarah Schultz, Nick Lee, Jack Campbell, Karen Athen
Series Cover Design: John Hamilton Design
Cover Photo: Veer

Printed in the United States of America
First Edition 2012

1 2 3 4 5 6 7 8 9 10

121311

# Contents

# Introduction to 1 Corinthians

## The Letter

Paul came to Corinth about the fall of AD 50 and founded the church, remaining there eighteen months (Acts 18:1–17). He then went to Ephesus (vv. 18–19).

Word that there were problems in the church led him to write a letter, which we do not have (1 Cor. 5:9). This "lost letter" must not have accomplished what he desired, because further word came to Paul from "Chloe's household" that there were serious problems in the Corinthian congregation (1 Cor. 1:11; 7:1; 16:17–18).

In response to this letter and the bad news he received, Paul wrote the letter we know as 1 Corinthians. He wrote it from Ephesus about AD 57.

## The Wisdom

The Christians in Corinth prided themselves in their spiritual gifts and knowledge. Yet something was radically wrong with their personal lives and with their local assembly.

Paul had what they needed—true spiritual wisdom. Not the wisdom of the world, but the wisdom that comes only from God.

We need this same wisdom today, and this letter is a good place to start discovering it. Paul's letter tells us how to be wise about the message and the ministry of the gospel, so that we will not get trapped into "fan clubs" for religious leaders. It tells us what kind of order we should have in our worship and how we should discover and develop our spiritual gifts. It also instructs us on how to keep our lives clean so that we glorify God and escape the pollutions of the world.

—*Warren W. Wiersbe*

# How to Use This Study

This study is designed for both individual and small-group use. We've divided it into eight lessons—each references one or more chapters in Warren W. Wiersbe's commentary *Be Wise* (second edition, David C Cook, 2010). While reading *Be Wise* is not a prerequisite for going through this study, the additional insights and background Wiersbe offers can greatly enhance your study experience.

The **Getting Started** questions at the beginning of each lesson offer you an opportunity to record your first thoughts and reactions to the study text. This is an important step in the study process as those "first impressions" often include clues about what it is your heart is longing to discover.

The bulk of the study is found in the **Going Deeper** questions. These dive into the Bible text and, along with helpful excerpts from Wiersbe's commentary, help you examine not only the original context and meaning of the verses but also modern application.

**Looking Inward** narrows the focus down to your personal story. These intimate questions can be a bit uncomfortable at times, but don't shy away from honesty here. This is where you are asked to stand before the mirror of God's Word and look closely at what you see. It's the place to take a good look at yourself in light of the lesson and search for ways in which you can grow in faith.

**Going Forward** is the place where you can commit to paper those things you want or need to do in order to better live out the discoveries you made in the Looking Inward section. Don't skip or skim through this. Take the time to really consider what practical steps you might take to move closer to Christ. Then share your thoughts with a trusted friend who can act as an encourager and accountability partner.

Finally, there is a brief **Seeking Help** section to close the lesson. This is a reminder for you to invite God into your spiritual-growth process. If you choose to write out a prayer in this section, come back to it as you work through the lesson and continue to seek the Holy Spirit's guidance as you discover God's will for your life.

## Tips for Small Groups

A small group is a dynamic thing. One week it might seem like a group of close-knit friends. The next it might seem more like a group of uncomfortable strangers. A small-group leader's role is to read these subtle changes and adjust the tone of the discussion accordingly.

Small groups need to be safe places for people to talk openly. It is through shared wrestling with difficult life issues that some of the greatest personal growth is discovered. But in order for the group to feel safe, participants need to know it's okay *not* to share sometimes. Always invite honest disclosure, but never force someone to speak if he or she isn't comfortable doing so. (A savvy leader will follow up later with a group member who isn't comfortable sharing in a group setting to see if a one-on-one discussion is more appropriate.)

Have volunteers take turns reading excerpts from Scripture or from the commentary. The more each person is involved even in the mundane tasks, the more they'll feel comfortable opening up in more meaningful ways.

The leader should watch the clock and keep the discussion moving. Sometimes there may be more Going Deeper questions than your group can cover in your available time. If you've had a fruitful discussion, it's okay to move on without finishing everything. And if you think the group is getting bogged down on a question or has taken off on a tangent, you can simply say, "Let's go on to question 5." Be sure to save at least ten to fifteen minutes for the Going Forward questions.

Finally, soak your group meetings in prayer—before you begin, during as needed, and always at the end of your time together.

# Calling and Message

## (1 CORINTHIANS 1—2)

*Before you begin ...*
- *Pray for the Holy Spirit to reveal truth and wisdom as you go through this lesson.*
- *Read 1 Corinthians 1—2. This lesson references chapters 1 and 2 in* Be Wise. *It will be helpful for you to have your Bible and a copy of the commentary available as you work through this lesson.*

## Getting Started

### From the Commentary

"Jesus, yes! The church, no!" This slogan was popular among young people in the '60s. They certainly could have used it with sincerity in Corinth back in AD 56, because the local church there was in serious trouble. Sad to say, the problems did not stay within the church family; they were known by the unbelievers outside the church.

To begin with, the church at Corinth was a *defiled* church. Some of its members were guilty of sexual immorality; others got drunk; still others were using the grace of God to excuse worldly living. It was also a *divided* church, with at least four different groups competing for leadership (1 Cor. 1:12). This meant it was a *disgraced* church. Instead of glorifying God, it was hindering the progress of the gospel.

—*Be Wise*, page 19

1. What caused the Corinthian church to fall into such disarray? What clues can we gather about this from the first part of Paul's letter? What are some of the typical root problems that cause a church to become "defiled"?

*More to Consider: Read Romans 1:18–32. Paul wrote the Roman epistle while in Corinth. What does this passage reveal about the Corinthian church?*

2. Choose one verse or phrase from 1 Corinthians 1—2 that stands out to you. This could be something you're intrigued by, something that makes

you uncomfortable, something that puzzles you, something that resonates with you, or just something you want to examine further. Write that here.

## Going Deeper

### From the Commentary

> Paul first attacked the serious problem of defilement in the church, yet he said nothing about the problem itself. Instead, he took the positive approach and reminded the believers of their high and holy position in Jesus Christ. In 1 Corinthians 1:1–9, he described the church that God sees; in 1 Corinthians 1:10–31, he described the church that men see. What we are in Jesus Christ *positionally* ought to be what we practice in daily life, but often we fail.
>
> —*Be Wise*, page 20

3. Review 1 Corinthians 1:1–9. What characteristics did Paul use to describe the church in these verses? According to Paul, what is the church's holy calling?

## From the Commentary

Having mentioned the problem of defilement in the church, now Paul turned to the matter of division in the church. Division has always been a problem among God's people, and almost every New Testament epistle deals with this topic or mentions it in one way or another. Even the twelve apostles did not always get along with each other.

In 1 Corinthians 1:13, Paul asked his readers three important questions, and these three questions are the key to this long paragraph.

(1) Is Christ divided (vv. 10–13a)?

(2) Were you baptized in the name of Paul (vv. 13b–17)?

(3) Was Paul crucified for you (vv. 18–25)?

—*Be Wise*, pages 22–24

4. Why did Paul ask these questions in 1 Corinthians 1:10–25? What do the answers reveal about the church? What are some of the causes of division in the church today?

## From the Commentary

> The Corinthians had a tendency to be "puffed up" with
> pride (1 Cor. 4:6, 18–19; 5:2). But the gospel of God's
> grace leaves no room for personal boasting. God is not
> impressed with our looks, our social position, our achieve-
> ments, our natural heritage, or our financial status. Note
> that Paul wrote *many*, not *any*. In the New Testament, we
> do meet some believers with "high social standing," but
> there are not many of them. The description Paul gave
> of the converts was certainly not a flattering one (1 Cor.
> 6:9–11).
>
> —*Be Wise*, page 27

5. Review 1 Corinthians 1:26–31. What did Paul mean when he wrote,
"God chose the foolish things of the world to shame the wise"? What are
the "weak" and "lowly" things he referred to? What does it look like to
boast in the Lord?

## From Today's World

Pride has always been an issue in the church, but today it has expanded beyond the walls of the local church into a sometimes-national phenomenon. When leaders in influential churches find success in publishing or blogging or speaking, they become the object of careful scrutiny by those inside and outside the church. With celebrity comes power, and with power comes the potential for abuse of that power.

6. How are the challenges facing churches and their leaders today different from those in the first-century church? How are they similar? What role does pride play in today's challenges? How can a church with a "celebrity status" avoid being puffed up with pride? What role does the congregation have in keeping the leadership humble?

## From the Commentary

Paul reminded the Corinthians of his approach (1 Cor. 2:1–2). The opening words, "And I," can be translated "Accordingly," on the basis of 1 Corinthians 1:31—the glory of God. Paul had not come to Corinth to glorify himself or to start a religious "fan club." He had come to glorify God.

The itinerant philosophers and teachers depended on their wisdom and eloquence to gain followers. The city of Corinth was filled with such "spellbinders." Paul did not depend on eloquent speech or clever arguments; he simply declared God's Word in the power of the Spirit. He was an ambassador, not a "Christian salesman."

Had he used spectacular speech and philosophy, Paul would have exalted himself and hidden the very Christ he came to proclaim! God had sent him to preach the gospel "not with wisdom of words, lest the cross of Christ should be made of none effect" (1 Cor. 1:17).

—*Be Wise*, page 34

7. How is Paul's approach to the church at Corinth (1 Cor. 2:1–5) like or unlike the way pastors deliver their messages today? Why is it so tempting to elevate oneself instead of Christ when preaching or speaking? How did Paul counter this?

## From the Commentary

> Salvation was purchased by the Son, but it was planned
> by the Father. Those who talk about "the simple gospel"
> are both right and wrong. Yes, the message of the gospel
> is simple enough for an illiterate pagan to understand,
> believe, and be saved. But it is also so profound that the
> most brilliant theologian cannot fathom its depths.
>
> There is a "wisdom of God" in the gospel that challenges
> the keenest intellect. However, this wisdom is not for the
> masses of lost sinners, nor is it for the immature believers.
> It is for the mature believers who are growing in their
> understanding of the Word of God. (The word *perfect* in
> 1 Corinthians 2:6 means "mature." See 1 Cor. 3:1–4.)
>
> —*Be Wise*, pages 36–37

8. What attitudes or beliefs might Paul have been responding to in
1 Corinthians 2:6–9? (See also Acts 18:24–28.) Why did he address the
issue of wisdom in this passage? What sort of wisdom might the church
have been following? Name some examples of secular wisdom today that
goes against God's wisdom.

*More to Consider: How might Paul have been referring to the spiritual and demonic "rulers of this present age"? (See John 12:31; 14:30; 16:11; Rom. 8:38; Col. 2:15; Eph. 6:12.)*

## From the Commentary

First Corinthians 2:9 is often used at funerals and applied to heaven, but the basic application is to the Christian's life *today*. The next verse makes it clear that God is revealing these things to us here and now.

This verse is a quotation (with adaptation) from Isaiah 64:4. The immediate context relates it to Israel in captivity, awaiting God's deliverance. The nation had sinned and had been sent to Babylon for chastening. They cried out to God that He would come down to deliver them, and He did answer their prayer after seventy years of their exile. God had plans for His people, and they did not have to be afraid (Jer. 29:11).

—*Be Wise*, page 39

9. How did Paul apply the principle in 1 Corinthians 2:9 to the church? Why is this an important message to a church that's in disarray? How is it applicable to today's church?

*From the Commentary*

Paul pointed out four important ministries of the Holy Spirit of God.

(1) The Spirit indwells believers (1 Cor. 2:12). The very moment you trusted Jesus Christ, the Spirit of God entered your body and made it His temple (1 Cor. 6:19–20). He baptized you (identified you) into the body of Christ (1 Cor. 12:13). He sealed you (Eph. 1:13–14) and will remain with you (John 14:16). He is God's gift to you.

(2) The Spirit searches (1 Cor. 2:10–11). I cannot know what is going on within your personality, but your human spirit within you knows. Neither can I know "the deep things of God" unless somehow I can enter into God's personality. I cannot do that—but by His Spirit, God has entered into my personality. Through the Holy Spirit, each believer becomes a sharer of the very life of God.

(3) The Spirit teaches (1 Cor. 2:13). Jesus promised that the Spirit would teach us (John 14:26) and guide us into truth (John 16:13). But we must note carefully the sequence here: The Spirit taught Paul from the Word, and Paul then taught the believers. The truth of God is found in the Word of God. And it is very important to note that these spiritual truths are given in specific *words*. In the Bible, we have much more than inspired thoughts; we have inspired *words*. "For I have given unto them the words which thou gavest me" (John 17:8).

(4) The Spirit matures the believer (1 Cor. 2:14–16). The contrast here is between the saved person (called "spiritual" because he is indwelt by the Spirit) and the unsaved person (called "natural" because he does not have the Spirit within). In 1 Corinthians 3:1–4, Paul will introduce a third kind of person, the "carnal man." He is the immature Christian, the one who lives on a childhood level because he will not feed on the Word and grow.

—*Be Wise*, pages 40–43

10. Review 1 Corinthians 2:10–16. Why did Paul focus these verses on the role of the Holy Spirit? What specific problems or challenges does this passage address? What does this passage tell you about Paul's understanding of the Corinthian church? In what ways does today's church face similar challenges?

## Looking Inward

Take a moment to reflect on all that you've explored thus far in this study of 1 Corinthians 1—2. Review your notes and answers and think about how each of these things matters in your life today.

*Tips for Small Groups: To get the most out of this section, form pairs or trios and have group members take turns answering these questions. Be honest and as open as you can in this discussion, but most of all, be encouraging and supportive of others. Be sensitive to those who are going through particularly difficult times and don't press for people to speak if they're uncomfortable doing so.*

11. What is your current perspective on the local church? What do you love about it? What do you not love? Do you feel connected to the church in healthy ways? If so, what are those ways? If not, where is the disconnect?

12. What are some ways you've struggled with pride? What puffs you up? How do you deal with these prideful moments? How do you respond when others are puffed up with pride? What is a Christlike response to others who are prideful?

13. What are the nonbiblical sources of wisdom you refer to? Do you test these against Scripture? What are the risks of trusting wisdom from somewhere other than God?

## Going Forward

14. Think of one or two things that you have learned that you'd like to work on in the coming week. Remember that this is all about quality, not quantity. It's better to work on one specific area of life and do it well than to work on many and do poorly (or to be so overwhelmed that you simply don't try).

Do you need to work on your pride or learn to trust God's wisdom? Be specific. Go back through 1 Corinthians 1—2 and put a star next to the phrase or verse that is most encouraging to you. Consider memorizing this verse.

*Real-Life Application Ideas: What are the key things your church exists to do (for example, worship God together, care for one another, help each other grow to maturity, care for outsiders)? Take a survey in your church to find out how well it is accomplishing those things. You can do this informally or formally, but look for clues to help you see what the church is doing well, and where it might need improvement. Share your results with church leadership, but focus mostly on what you can do to help your church fulfill its mission.*

## Seeking Help

15. Write a prayer below (or simply pray one in silence), inviting God to work on your mind and heart in those areas you've noted in the Going Forward section. Be honest about your desires and fears.

*Notes for Small Groups:*

- *Look for ways to put into practice the things you wrote in the Going Forward section. Talk with other group members about your ideas and commit to being accountable to one another.*

- *During the coming week, ask the Holy Spirit to continue to reveal truth to you from what you've read and studied.*

- *Before you start the next lesson, read 1 Corinthians 3—4. For more in-depth lesson preparation, read chapters 3 and 4, "Be Wise about the Local Church" and "Be Wise about the Christian Ministry," in* Be Wise.

# The Church
## (1 CORINTHIANS 3—4)

*Before you begin …*
- *Pray for the Holy Spirit to reveal truth and wisdom as you go through this lesson.*
- *Read 1 Corinthians 3—4. This lesson references chapters 3 and 4 in* Be Wise. *It will be helpful for you to have your Bible and a copy of the commentary available as you work through this lesson.*

## Getting Started

*From the Commentary*

Paul already explained that there are two kinds of people in the world—natural (unsaved) and spiritual (saved). But now he explained that there are two kinds of saved people: mature and immature (carnal). A Christian matures by allowing the Spirit to teach him and direct him by feeding on the Word. The immature Christian lives for the things of the flesh (*carnal* means "flesh") and has little interest in the things of the Spirit. Of course, some believers are immature because they have been saved only a short time, but that is not what Paul was discussing here.

Paul was the "spiritual father" who brought this family into being (1 Cor. 4:15). During the eighteen months he ministered in Corinth, Paul had tried to feed his spiritual children and help them mature in the faith. Just as in a human family, everybody helps the new baby grow and mature, so in the family of God we must encourage spiritual maturity.

—*Be Wise*, pages 47–48

1. What is Paul's theme in 1 Corinthians 3:1–4? What are the marks of Christian maturity that the Corinthians lacked? How is maturity different from knowledge of the Bible alone?

*More to Consider: Read the following: 1 Peter 2:2; Matthew 4:4; Hebrews 5:11–14; and Psalm 119:103. How do these passages use the metaphor of food to describe a balanced spiritual diet?*

2. Choose one verse or phrase from 1 Corinthians 3—4 that stands out to you. This could be something you're intrigued by, something that makes you uncomfortable, something that puzzles you, something that resonates with you, or just something you want to examine further. Write that here.

# Going Deeper

*From the Commentary*

> Paul was fond of agricultural images and often used them in his letters. "Ye are God's husbandry" simply means, "You are God's cultivated field, God's garden." In the parable of the sower, Jesus compared the human heart to soil and the Word of God to seed (Matt. 13:1–9, 18–23). Paul took this *individual* image and made it *collective*: The local church is a field that ought to bear fruit. The task of the ministry is the sowing of the seed, the cultivating of the soil, the watering of the plants, and the harvesting of the fruit.
>
> —*Be Wise*, page 50

3. Review 1 Corinthians 3:5–9. Why did Paul choose this particular imagery to make his point? How did the image of the church as a "field" apply to the specific problems in the Corinthian church? How might it apply to churches today?

## From the Commentary

> God wants to see increase in His field…. Along with spiritual growth, there should be a measure of numerical growth. *Fruit has in it the seed for more fruit.* If the fruit of our ministry is genuine, it will eventually produce "more fruit … much fruit" to the glory of God (John 15:1–8).
>
> Those who serve in ministry must constantly be caring for the "soil" of the church. It requires diligence and hard work to produce a harvest. The lazy preacher or Sunday school teacher is like the slothful farmer Solomon wrote about in Proverbs 24:30–34. Satan is busy sowing discord, lies, and sin; and we must be busy cultivating the soil and planting the good seed of the Word of God.
>
> —*Be Wise*, page 52

4. Paul encouraged the Corinthian church as he did many other churches, challenging them to produce the fruit that comes with maturity. Read Romans 1:13; 6:22; 15:26–28; Galatians 5:22–23; Colossians 1:10; and Hebrews 13:15. What fruits or harvest do these passages describe? How do you know when a church is producing these fruits?

## From the Commentary

The usual explanation of 1 Corinthians 3:9–23 is that it describes the building of the Christian life. We all build on Christ, but some people use good materials, while others use poor materials. The kind of material you use determines the kind of reward you will get.

While this may be a valid *application* of this passage, it is not the basic *interpretation*. Paul was discussing the building of the local church, the temple of God. (In 1 Corinthians 6:19–20, the individual believer is God's temple; but here it is the local assembly that is in view. In Ephesians 2:19–22, the whole church is compared to a temple of God.) Paul pointed out that one day God will judge our labors as related to the local assembly. "The fire will test the quality of each man's work" (1 Cor. 3:13 NIV).

God is concerned that we build with quality. The church does not belong to the preacher or to the congregation. It is *God's* church. "Ye are God's building" (1 Cor. 3:9). If we are going to build the local church the way God wants it built, we must meet certain conditions.

—*Be Wise*, pages 52–53

5. According to 1 Corinthians 3:9–23, what are the conditions we must meet to build a church God's way? What does it mean to "build with quality"? What are some clues that tell us when a church is being built to satisfy the preacher or the congregation instead of God? How do we go about changing that?

### From the Commentary

The members of the Corinthian church were glorying in men, and this was wrong. They were comparing men (1 Cor. 4:6) and dividing the church by such carnal deeds. Had they been seeking to glorify God alone, there would have been harmony in the assembly.

No member of the church should say, "I belong to Paul!"

or "I like Peter!" because each servant belongs to each member equally. Perhaps we cannot help but have our personal preferences when it comes to the way different men minister the Word. But we must not permit our personal preferences to become divisive prejudices. In fact, the preacher I may enjoy the least may be the one I need the most!

—*Be Wise*, page 57

6. Review 1 Corinthians 3:21–23. Why was motive so important to Paul? Why did Paul close this section by pointing out that each believer possesses all things in Christ? How did this address the problem of church members who were aligning themselves with individuals instead of with Christ?

## From the Commentary

In 1 Corinthians 3, Paul presented three pictures of the local church. Now he presents three pictures of the minister—a steward (1 Cor. 4:1–6), a spectacle (1 Cor. 4:7–13), and a father (1 Cor. 4:14–21). He wanted his readers to understand how God measures and evaluates a Christian's service. First Corinthians 4:6 explains Paul's purpose: "That no one of you be puffed up for one against another."

—*Be Wise*, page 61

7. Why is it important to avoid being too critical when evaluating people and their ministries? Why is it important to avoid being too lax when doing so? How did Paul address these extremes of evaluation in 1 Corinthians 4? Read 1 John 4:1–6 and 2 John. What do these passages tell us about how to evaluate ministry?

## From the Commentary

Paul answered the leaders of the various factions in the church when he called himself, Peter, and Apollos "ministers of Christ." The word translated "ministers" is literally "under-rowers." It described the slaves who rowed the huge Roman galleys. "We are not the captains of the ship," said Paul, "but only the galley slaves who are under orders. Now, is one slave greater than another?"

Then Paul explained the image of the *steward*. A steward is a servant who manages everything for his master, but who himself owns nothing. Joseph was a chief steward in Potiphar's household (Gen. 39). The church is the "household of faith" (Gal. 6:10), and the ministers are stewards who share God's wealth with the family (Matt. 13:52). Paul called this spiritual wealth "the mysteries of God." We met this important word *mystery* in 1 Corinthians 2:7, so you may want to review it.

So, the main issue is not, "Is Paul popular?" or, "Is Apollos a better preacher than Paul?" The main issue is, "Have Paul, Apollos, and Peter been faithful to do the work God assigned to them?"

—*Be Wise*, pages 61–62

8. Why did Paul focus on the imagery of the steward in 1 Corinthians 4? What is the responsibility of a steward? (See also Rom. 14:4.) How does this passage deal with the issue of popularity? Why was that important to the Corinthian church? How is it important today?

*More to Consider: Read 1 Samuel 12:1–5 and Acts 20:17–38. How do these passages demonstrate Samuel's and Paul's faithfulness? How can these examples help us as we evaluate leaders and ministers today?*

## From the Commentary

When Paul called himself and other apostles "a spectacle unto the world" (1 Cor. 4:9), he was using an image familiar to people in the Roman Empire. The government kept the people pacified by presenting entertainments in the different cities. The amphitheaters would be filled with citizens, eager to see men compete in the games and prisoners fight with the beasts. (In fact, the Greek word translated "spectacle" gives us our English word *theater*.) The Coliseum at Rome became the center for these "entertainments."

When the "main events" were ended, then the poorest and weakest prisoners were brought in to fight with the beasts. Nobody expected too much from their performance.

What a picture of the apostles of Jesus Christ!

—*Be Wise*, pages 64–65

9. Review 1 Corinthians 4:7–13. Circle the contrasts Paul made in these verses. What is the purpose of these contrasts? In what ways might they have humbled the Corinthians? Why was this important?

## From the Commentary

> Paul had already compared the local church to a family
> (1 Cor. 3:1–4). But now the emphasis is on the minis-
> ter as a "spiritual father." In none of his letters did Paul
> ever call himself "father." He was mindful of the Lord's
> teaching in Matthew 23:8–12. But in comparing himself
> to a "spiritual father," Paul reminded the church of the
> important ministries he had performed on their behalf.
>
> First, Paul had founded the family (1 Cor. 4:14–15).
>
> Second, Paul was an example to the family (1 Cor.
> 4:16–17).
>
> Third, Paul was faithful to discipline the family (1 Cor.
> 4:18–21).
>
> —*Be Wise*, pages 67–69

10. Why was it important for Paul to remind the church of the ministries
he had performed? How would the church have received this? How is this
different from being puffed up with pride?

## Looking Inward

Take a moment to reflect on all that you've explored thus far in this study of 1 Corinthians 3—4. Review your notes and answers and think about how each of these things matters in your life today.

*Tips for Small Groups: To get the most out of this section, form pairs or trios and have group members take turns answering these questions. Be honest and as open as you can in this discussion, but most of all, be encouraging and supportive of others. Be sensitive to those who are going through particularly difficult times and don't press for people to speak if they're uncomfortable doing so.*

11. How would you describe your current level of spiritual maturity? What are some ways you've intentionally worked on becoming more mature? What are some areas of your spiritual life where you feel you need to grow? How will you work on those?

12. Have you ever put more faith in a leader than you ought? What was the result of that experience? Why is it so tempting to glorify people instead of God? If you've ever been in a leadership position, how did you deal with the temptation to be prideful?

13. In what ways are you a steward of God's love? How can you develop that quality?

## Going Forward

14. Think of one or two things that you have learned that you'd like to work on in the coming week. Remember that this is all about quality, not quantity. It's better to work on one specific area of life and do it well than to work on many and do poorly (or to be so overwhelmed that you simply don't try).

Do you need to work on developing your spiritual maturity? Be specific. Go back through 1 Corinthians 3—4 and put a star next to the phrase or verse that is most encouraging to you. Consider memorizing this verse.

*Real-Life Application Ideas: Write a brief history of your faith journey so far. Note the events and circumstances that were most significant to your spiritual growth along the way. After taking time to thank God for how far He's brought you, look ahead and set goals for further growing in your faith. List specific ways you plan to work on this in the future, then make a commitment to pursue those goals with diligence.*

## Seeking Help

15. Write a prayer below (or simply pray one in silence), inviting God to work on your mind and heart in those areas you've noted in the Going Forward section. Be honest about your desires and fears.

*Notes for Small Groups:*

- *Look for ways to put into practice the things you wrote in the Going Forward section. Talk with other group members about your ideas and commit to being accountable to one another.*

- *During the coming week, ask the Holy Spirit to continue to reveal truth to you from what you've read and studied.*

- *Before you start the next lesson, read 1 Corinthians 5—6. For more in-depth lesson preparation, read chapter 5, "Be Wise about Church Discipline," in* Be Wise.

# Discipline
## (1 CORINTHIANS 5—6)

*Before you begin …*
- *Pray for the Holy Spirit to reveal truth and wisdom as you go through this lesson.*
- *Read 1 Corinthians 5—6. This lesson references chapter 5 in Be Wise. It will be helpful for you to have your Bible and a copy of the commentary available as you work through this lesson.*

## Getting Started

*From the Commentary*

The church at Corinth was not only a divided church, but it was also a disgraced church. There was sin in the assembly and, sad to say, everybody knew about it. But the church was slow to *do* anything about it.

No church is perfect, but human imperfection must never be an excuse for sin. Just as parents must discipline their children in love, so local churches must exercise discipline over the members of the assembly. Church discipline is not a group of "pious policemen" out to catch a criminal. Rather, it is a group of brokenhearted brothers and sisters seeking to restore an erring member of the family.

—*Be Wise*, page 73

1. Why is church discipline such a touchy subject for churches today? What are the greatest challenges facing a church that needs to be disciplined for inappropriate behavior or teaching? Whose responsibility is it to speak out when a church is getting off track?

2. Choose one verse or phrase from 1 Corinthians 5—6 that stands out to you. This could be something you're intrigued by, something that makes you uncomfortable, something that puzzles you, something that resonates with you, or just something you want to examine further. Write that here.

# Going Deeper

*From the Commentary*

> "What will this sin do to the church?" is certainly an
> important consideration. Christians are "called to be
> saints" (1 Cor. 1:2), and this means holy living to the
> glory of God. If a Christian loves his church, he will not
> stand by and permit sin to weaken it and perhaps ruin its
> testimony.
>
> —*Be Wise*, page 73

3. Review 1 Corinthians 5. What is the specific sin addressed in this passage?
What is the significance of Paul's comment that this sin is something even
pagans do not tolerate? How did Paul address this sin?

*More to Consider: Review Leviticus 18:6–8; 20:11. What do these
passages tell us about the sin in question? Why didn't Paul pass
judgment on the woman in this story?*

## From the Commentary

While Christians are not to judge one another's motives (Matt. 7:1–5) or ministries (1 Cor. 4:5), we are certainly expected to be honest about each other's conduct. In my own pastoral ministry, I have never enjoyed having to initiate church discipline; but since it is commanded in the Scriptures, we must obey God and set personal feelings aside.

Paul described here an official church meeting at which the offender was dealt with according to divine instructions. Public sin must be publicly judged and condemned. (For our Lord's instructions about discipline, study Matt. 18:15–20.) The sin was not to be swept under the rug; for, after all, it was known far and wide even among the unsaved who were outside the church.

The church was to gather together and expel the offender. Note the strong words that Paul used to instruct them: "taken away from among you" (1 Cor. 5:2), "deliver such an one unto Satan" (1 Cor. 5:5), "purge out" (1 Cor. 5:7), and "put away" (1 Cor. 5:13). Paul did not suggest that they handle the offender gently. Of course, we assume that first the spiritual leaders of the church sought to restore the man personally.

*—Be Wise*, pages 74–75

4. How did Paul go about directing the church to deal with the sin? What does it mean to deliver a Christian "unto Satan"? By what authority is

sin dealt with in the church? Why is it so important not to treat church members' behavior lightly or carelessly?

## From Today's World

In a media-saturated world, things that used to be the fodder for rumor mills and hearsay have become as significant as hard news. The "breaking news" of today could as easily be about a sex scandal as a devastating hurricane or tsunami. When the person in question is a public figure—usually in politics or entertainment—the level of coverage is often astonishing. The same thing happens on a much smaller scale in today's churches. People are quick to share rumors and truths about bad behavior or actions through social media, which has taken the place of the telephone as the means for sharing information, whether true or not.

5. How is the way the media deal with scandal and public sin like and unlike the way the church deals with it? What is it about someone else's sins that makes the subject so tempting to share with others? What are healthy ways for the church to deal with members who are in obvious sin? What about those who are rumored to be in sin? Why is this such a touchy subject for churches to deal with?

*From the Commentary*

> The image here is that of the Passover supper (Ex. 12).
> Jesus is the Lamb of God who shed His blood to deliver
> us from sin (John 1:29; 1 Peter 1:18–25). The Jews in
> Egypt were delivered from death by the application of
> the blood of the lamb. Following the application of the
> blood, the Jewish families ate the Passover supper. One
> of the requirements was that no yeast (leaven) be found
> anywhere in their dwellings. Even the bread at the feast
> was to be unleavened.
>
> Leaven is a picture of sin. It is small but powerful; it works
> secretly; it "puffs up" the dough; it spreads. The sinning
> church member in Corinth was like a piece of yeast: He
> was defiling the entire loaf of bread (the congregation). It
> was like a cancer in the body that needed to be removed
> by drastic surgery.
>
> The church must purge itself of "old leaven"—the things
> that belong to the "old life" before we trusted Christ. We
> must also get rid of malice and wickedness (there was
> a great deal of hard feelings between members of the
> Corinthian church) and replace them with sincerity and
> truth. As a loaf of bread (1 Cor. 10:17), the local church
> must be as pure as possible.
>
> —*Be Wise*, pages 75–76

6. Review 1 Corinthians 5:6–13. What are examples of sin as "leaven"
that the early church dealt with? How is the church dealing with the same

issues today? How should the church purge itself of "old leaven"? What if the person in sin is in a leadership position? How should the church proceed? Who determines what sins are significant enough to confront?

## From the Commentary

The church at Corinth was rapidly losing its testimony in the city. Not only did the unsaved know about the immorality in the assembly, but they were also aware of the lawsuits involving members of the church. Not only were there sins of the flesh, but also sins of the spirit (2 Cor. 7:1).

Paul detected three tragedies in this situation.

First, the believers were presenting a poor testimony to the lost.

Second, the congregation had failed to live up to its full position in Christ.

There was a third tragedy: The members suing each other had already lost. Even if some of them won their

cases, they had incurred a far greater loss in their dis-
obedience to the Word of God.

—*Be Wise*, pages 76–78

7. Why were lawsuits such a contentious issue in the Corinthian church?
What do you make of Paul's statement in 1 Corinthians 6:4? When is it
wrong for Christians to take their civil suits to court, and why? How does
this apply today (or does it)?

## From the Commentary

There was a great deal of sexual laxness in the city of
Corinth. It was a permissive society with a philosophy
similar to that which the world has today: Sex is a normal
physical function, so why not use it as you please? Paul
pointed out that God created sex when He made the first
man and woman, and therefore He has the right to tell us
how to use it. The Bible is the "owner's manual," and it
must be obeyed.

God condemns sexual sins; Paul named some of them
in 1 Corinthians 6:9. In that day, idolatry and sensuality
went together.

—*Be Wise*, page 78

8. Review 1 Corinthians 6:9–20. Why do you suppose the Corinthian
church was so lax regarding sexual matters? Why is this true in society
today? Why do you think Paul linked idolatry and sensuality? In what
ways might that still be true today?

*More to Consider: Read Romans 1:26–27. What did Paul confront
in this passage? How do his words apply to believers today? What role
(if any) does culture play in Paul's condemnation of specific sexual sin?*

### From the Commentary

God the Father created our bodies, and one day He will
resurrect them in glory. (More about the resurrection in
1 Corinthians 15.) In view of the fact that our bodies

have such a wonderful origin, and an even more wonderful future, how can we use them for such evil purposes?

The Corinthians had two arguments to defend their sensuality. First, "All things are lawful unto me" (1 Cor. 6:12). This was a popular phrase in Corinth, based on a false view of Christian freedom. We have not been set free so that we can enter into a new kind of bondage! As Christians, we must ask ourselves, "Will this enslave me? Is this activity really profitable for my spiritual life?"

Their second argument was, "Meats for the belly, and the belly for meats" (1 Cor. 6:13). They treated sex as an appetite to be satisfied and not as a gift to be cherished and used carefully. Sensuality is to sex what gluttony is to eating; both are sinful and both bring disastrous consequences. Just because we have certain normal desires, given by God at creation, does not mean that we must give in to them and always satisfy them. Sex outside of marriage is destructive, while sex in marriage can be creative and beautiful.

—*Be Wise*, page 79

9. How are the arguments the Corinthian Christians gave about why they indulged in sexual immorality like the sorts of arguments people make today? (See 1 Cor. 6:13.) What would Paul say makes sex outside of marriage so destructive? Why do you think Paul spent so much time addressing this topic? What does that say about the Corinthians? About Paul?

## From the Commentary

As you review this section, you will see that sexual sins affect the entire personality. They affect the *emotions*, leading to slavery (1 Cor. 6:12b). It is frightening to see how sensuality can get a hold of a person and defile his entire life, enslaving him to habits that destroy. It also affects a person *physically* (1 Cor. 6:18). The fornicator and adulterer, as well as the homosexual, may forget their sins, *but their sins will not forget them.*

In my pastoral counseling, I have had to help married couples whose relationship was falling apart because of the consequences of *pre*marital sex, as well as *extra*marital sex. The harvest of sowing to the flesh is sometimes delayed, but it is certain (Gal. 6:7–8). How sad it is to live with the consequences of *forgiven* sin.

Having said all this, we must also realize that there are *eternal* consequences for people who practice sexual sins.… A Christian may fall into these sins and be forgiven, as was David; but no Christian would *practice* such sins (1 John 3:1–10).

Finally, in all fairness, we must note that there are other sins besides sexual sins. For some reason, the church has often majored on condemning the sins of the Prodigal Son and has forgotten the sins of the elder brother (Luke 15:11–32). There are sins of the spirit as well as sins of the flesh—Paul names some of them in 1 Corinthians 6:10.

Covetousness can send a man to hell just as easily as can
adultery.

—*Be Wise*, pages 81–82

10. What bold statement about God's kingdom did Paul make in
1 Corinthians 6:9–10? What sort of response might this have garnered
from the Corinthian Christians? What other sins (besides sexual sins) did
Paul single out that can strip people of the kingdom? What's the difference
between someone living a life of sin and a person who has sinned but been
forgiven?

## Looking Inward

Take a moment to reflect on all that you've explored thus far in this study
of 1 Corinthians 5—6. Review your notes and answers and think about
how each of these things matters in your life today.

*Tips for Small Groups: To get the most out of this section, form pairs or trios and have group members take turns answering these questions. Be honest and as open as you can in this discussion, but most of all, be encouraging and supportive of others. Be sensitive to those who are going through particularly difficult times and don't press for people to speak if they're uncomfortable doing so.*

11. Have you ever had to call out a fellow believer because of his or her sin? Without being too specific, what was that experience like? What was the result of the confrontation?

12. Have you ever been the object of church discipline? If so, describe that experience. In what ways did you grow from the experience? What was difficult about it?

13. If you've struggled with sexual sin or immorality, take a few moments to think about what led to those struggles. You don't need to write anything down here, but how did you (or do you still) deal with those issues? Are there some things you should be doing, but aren't, to confront these areas of your life? What are they? What's holding you back?

## Going Forward

14. Think of one or two things that you have learned that you'd like to work on in the coming week. Remember that this is all about quality, not quantity. It's better to work on one specific area of life and do it well than to work on many and do poorly (or to be so overwhelmed that you simply don't try).

Do you need to deal with an issue of discipline in your church? Be specific. Go back through 1 Corinthians 5—6 and put a star next to the phrase or verse that is most encouraging to you. Consider memorizing this verse.

> *Real-Life Application Ideas: Does your church have an established policy for dealing with both sin in the church and rumors of sin? Talk with church leaders about this. If your church doesn't have a specific policy, work with leaders to establish one. It's important for churches to be prepared to confront the negative power of rumors as well as the potential devastation that comes from unchecked sin within its membership.*

## Seeking Help

15. Write a prayer below (or simply pray one in silence), inviting God to work on your mind and heart in those areas you've noted in the Going Forward section. Be honest about your desires and fears.

*Notes for Small Groups:*

- *Look for ways to put into practice the things you wrote in the Going Forward section. Talk with other group members about your ideas and commit to being accountable to one another.*

- *During the coming week, ask the Holy Spirit to continue to reveal truth to you from what you've read and studied.*

- *Before you start the next lesson, read 1 Corinthians 7. For more in-depth lesson preparation, read chapter 6, "Be Wise about Christian Marriage," in* Be Wise.

# Marriage
## (I CORINTHIANS 7)

*Before you begin ...*
- *Pray for the Holy Spirit to reveal truth and wisdom as you go through this lesson.*
- *Read 1 Corinthians 7. This lesson references chapter 6 in Be Wise. It will be helpful for you to have your Bible and a copy of the commentary available as you work through this lesson.*

## Getting Started

### From the Commentary

Up to this point, Paul had been dealing with the sins reported to be known in the Corinthian congregation. Now he takes up the questions about which they had written to him: marriage (1 Cor. 7:1, 25), food offered to idols (1 Cor. 8:1), spiritual gifts (1 Cor. 12:1), the resurrection of the dead (1 Cor. 15:1), and the missionary offering for the Jews (1 Cor. 16:1).

—*Be Wise*, page 85

1. Why is it important to note that Paul was responding to specific questions and not outlining an entire theology about marriage? What sort of misinterpretation could result from considering the message in 1 Corinthians 7 as a complete theology? What's missing?

*More to Consider: Review 1 Corinthians 7:6, 10, 12, and 25. Why might some readers believe he was disclaiming divine inspiration for this content? How was Paul's message similar to what Jesus taught in Matthew 5:31–32; 19:1–12; Mark 10:1–12; Luke 16:18? Why is this significant in the context of Paul's letter?*

2. Choose one verse or phrase from 1 Corinthians 7 that stands out to you. This could be something you're intrigued by, something that makes you uncomfortable, something that puzzles you, something that resonates with you, or just something you want to examine further. Write that here.

# Going Deeper

*From the Commentary*

> Apparently one of the questions the church asked was, "Is
> celibacy [remaining unmarried and abstaining from sex]
> more spiritual than marriage?" Paul replied that it is good
> for a man or a woman to have the gift of celibacy, but the
> celibate state is not better than marriage, nor is it the best
> state for everybody. Dr. Kenneth Wuest translated Paul's
> reply, "It is perfectly proper, honorable, morally befitting
> for a man to live in strict celibacy."
>
> —*Be Wise*, page 86

3. Review 1 Corinthians 7:1–11. What is the core question Paul addressed in
these verses? How does this passage tie in with Jesus' teaching in Matthew
19:10–12? In what ways does Genesis 2:18 play into this discussion?

*From the Commentary*

> As in all things, the spiritual must govern the physical;
> for our bodies are God's temples. The husband and wife

may abstain in order to devote their full interest to prayer and fasting (1 Cor. 7:5); but they must not use this as an excuse for prolonged separation. Paul is encouraging Christian partners to be "in tune" with each other in matters both spiritual and physical.

—*Be Wise*, page 87

4. How did Paul apply the principle stated in 1 Corinthians 7:1 to single believers and widows in 7:8–9? Do you believe the argument Paul gave: "If you can't control yourself" is a good reason to marry? Why or why not? What is the deeper spiritual truth being championed here?

## From Today's World

Marriage is a sacred thing to Christians and has been for centuries. However, in recent years, the very definition of marriage has been challenged in the courts by those who want to expand the long-held belief that marriage is solely a union between one man and one woman. As states across the nation wrestle with this question at the ballot box, believers must wrestle with its implications in the local community as well as in their hearts.

5. Why do you think marriage has become such a contentious subject in our world today? What is it about the Bible's definition of marriage that troubles so many other people? Should the state governments give in to these pressures? What is lost by doing this? Is anything gained? How are Christians to respond when marriage is redefined in the courts?

## From the Commentary

Not only did the church ask about celibacy, but they also asked Paul about divorce. Since Jesus had dealt with this question, Paul cited His teaching: Husbands and wives are not to divorce each other (see also 1 Cor. 7:39). If divorce does occur, the parties should remain unmarried or seek reconciliation.

This is, of course, the ideal for marriage. Jesus did make one exception: If one party was guilty of fornication, this could be grounds for divorce. Far better that there be confession, forgiveness, and reconciliation; but if these are out of the question, then the innocent party may get a divorce. However, divorce is the last option; first, every means available should be used to restore the marriage.

—*Be Wise*, page 87

6. Divorce is obviously a much bigger topic for discussion today than it was in Paul's time. How are the two cultures different? How is Paul's teaching (based on Jesus' teaching) as valid for today as it was then? Why do you think there is so much divorce in the church today? How can the church address this important issue better?

## From the Commentary

Some of the members of the Corinthian church were saved after they had been married, but their mates had not yet been converted. No doubt, some of these believers were having a difficult time at home; and they asked Paul, "Must we remain married to unsaved partners? Doesn't our conversion alter things?"

Paul replied that they were to remain with their unconverted mates so long as their mates were willing to live with them. Salvation does not alter the marriage state; if anything, it ought to enhance the marriage relationship. (Note Peter's counsel to wives with unsaved husbands in 1 Peter 3:1–6.) Since marriage is basically a physical relationship ("they shall be one flesh," Gen. 2:24), it can only be broken by a physical cause. Adultery and death would be two such causes (1 Cor. 7:39).

—*Be Wise*, pages 87–88

7. Review 1 Corinthians 7:12–24. What does this passage say about Christians who choose to marry nonbelievers? Why was this such a big deal to Paul? Is it still a big deal today? Why or why not? What are the risks of marrying a nonbeliever?

## From the Commentary

Suppose an unsaved mate leaves the home? First Corinthians 7:15 gives the answer: The Christian partner is not obligated to keep the home together. We are called to peace, and we should do all we can to live in peace (Rom. 12:18); but there comes a time in some situations where peace is impossible. If the unsaved mate separates from his or her partner, there is little the Christian can do except to pray and continue to be faithful to the Lord.

Does separation then give the Christian mate the right to divorce and remarry? Paul did not say so. What if the unconverted mate ends up living with another partner? That would constitute adultery and give grounds for divorce.

—*Be Wise*, page 89

8. In what ways are Paul's answers about marriage all about spiritual principles, not rules? How does this affect the way we interpret passages such as 1 Corinthians 7:15? What role does forgiveness play in all of this? (See 7:10–11.)

## From the Commentary

It was a time of distress (1 Cor. 7:26) when society was going through change (1 Cor. 7:31). There was not much time left for serving the Lord (1 Cor. 7:29). It is possible that there were political and economic pressures in Corinth about which we have no information. In view of the difficulties, it would be better for a person to be unmarried. However, this did not mean that married people should seek a divorce (1 Cor. 7:27). Paul's counsel was to the unmarried.

This did not mean that *nobody* should get married; but those who do marry must be ready to accept the trials that will accompany it (1 Cor. 7:28). In fact, the situation might become so difficult that even those already married will have to live as though they were not married (1 Cor. 7:29). Perhaps Paul was referring to husbands and wives being separated from each other because of economic distress or persecution.

—*Be Wise*, page 90

9. What does 1 Corinthians 7:25–31 tell us about context and its impact on decision making? What sort of present crisis today might be enough reason for believers to decide it's better not to be married? What is the overall message to believers about marriage in this passage?

## From the Commentary

Finally, remember that marriage is for life (1 Cor. 7:39–40). It is God's will that the marriage union be permanent, a lifetime commitment. There is no place in Christian marriage for a "trial marriage," nor is there any room for the "escape hatch" attitude: "If the marriage doesn't work, we can always get a divorce."

For this reason, marriage must be built on something sturdier than good looks, money, romantic excitement, and social acceptance. There must be Christian commitment, character, and maturity. There must be a willingness to grow, to learn from each other, to forgive and forget, to minister to one another. The kind of love Paul described in 1 Corinthians 13 is what is needed to cement two lives together.

—*Be Wise*, page 93

10. Why is the "marriage is for life" message so strong in Paul's letter? How is that message still taught today? Why, then, is divorce still so common among Christians? What cements a Christian marriage?

## Looking Inward

Take a moment to reflect on all that you've explored thus far in this study of 1 Corinthians 7. Review your notes and answers and think about how each of these things matters in your life today.

*Tips for Small Groups: To get the most out of this section, form pairs or trios and have group members take turns answering these questions. Be honest and as open as you can in this discussion, but most of all, be encouraging and supportive of others. Be sensitive to those who are going through particularly difficult times and don't press for people to speak if they're uncomfortable doing so.*

11. If you've never been married, is it because you've chosen this or because you haven't yet found the right mate? What appeals to you about singleness? About marriage? How easy is it to remain celibate as a single person in today's society? Why?

12. If you're married, how does Paul's advice in 1 Corinthians 7 resonate (or not) with you? What are some ways you see your marriage as a positive thing? What are the greatest challenges you face in your marriage? How can you work together to assure that your marriage is "for life"?

13. How has your life been affected by divorce? Perhaps your parents were divorced, or you were, or some close friends. How do you respond to friends who are struggling in their marriage? Are there ever good reasons for divorce beyond those Paul talked about in 1 Corinthians? If so, what are they and how can you justify them biblically?

## Going Forward

14. Think of one or two things that you have learned that you'd like to work on in the coming week. Remember that this is all about quality, not quantity. It's better to work on one specific area of life and do it well than to work on many and do poorly (or to be so overwhelmed that you simply don't try).

Do you need to work toward a better understanding of what it means to be married? Be specific. Go back through 1 Corinthians 7 and put a star next to the phrase or verse that is most encouraging to you. Consider memorizing this verse.

*Real-Life Application Ideas: Attend a marriage seminar (if you're married) or one on relationships for singles (if you're not). Use this time to really study what the Bible teaches about marriage and relationships so you can make wise decisions. Don't be shy about this—it's not always easy to attend one of these events, but it's usually worth it.*

## Seeking Help

15. Write a prayer below (or simply pray one in silence), inviting God to work on your mind and heart in those areas you've noted in the Going Forward section. Be honest about your desires and fears.

*Notes for Small Groups:*

- *Look for ways to put into practice the things you wrote in the Going Forward section. Talk with other group members about your ideas and commit to being accountable to one another.*

- *During the coming week, ask the Holy Spirit to continue to reveal truth to you from what you've read and studied.*

- *Before you start the next lesson, read 1 Corinthians 8—10. For more in-depth lesson preparation, read chapters 7 and 8, "Be Wise about Christian Liberty" and "Be Wise about Personal Priorities," in* Be Wise.

# Liberty
## (I CORINTHIANS 8—10)

*Before you begin ...*
- *Pray for the Holy Spirit to reveal truth and wisdom as you go through this lesson.*
- *Read 1 Corinthians 8—10. This lesson references chapters 7 and 8 in* Be Wise. *It will be helpful for you to have your Bible and a copy of the commentary available as you work through this lesson.*

## Getting Started

*From the Commentary*

After answering their questions about marriage, Paul turned to one of the most controversial subjects in the letter he received from the Corinthian church: "Can Christians eat meat that has been sacrificed to idols?" The immediate question does not interest believers today since we do not face that problem. But the wider issue of "Christian liberty" *does* apply to us, because we face questions that Paul never faced. Is it right for Christians to attend the theater? Should a believer have a television set in his home? To what extent can a Christian get involved in politics?

In 1 Corinthians 8—10, Paul enunciated four basic principles that would guide believers in making personal decisions about those "questionable" areas of the Christian life.

—*Be Wise*, page 97

1. What is liberty, according to Paul? Why is it an important topic for discussion within the church? What principles did Paul outline in 1 Corinthians 8—10 regarding liberty?

*More to Consider: Paul addressed himself primarily to the strong Christians in the church. Why did he focus his energies here? (See Rom. 14—15.)*

2. Choose one verse or phrase from 1 Corinthians 8—10 that stands out to you. This could be something you're intrigued by, something that makes

you uncomfortable, something that puzzles you, something that resonates with you, or just something you want to examine further. Write that here.

## Going Deeper

*From the Commentary*

There were two sources of meat in the ancient world: the regular market (where the prices were higher) and the local temples (where meat from the sacrifices was always available). The strong members of the church realized that idols could not contaminate food, so they saved money by purchasing the cheaper meat available from the temples. Furthermore, if unconverted friends invited them to a feast at which sacrificial meat was served, the strong Christians attended it whether at the temple or in the home.

All of this offended the weaker Christians. Many of them had been saved out of pagan idolatry, and they could not understand why their fellow believers would want to have anything to do with meat sacrificed to idols. (In Romans 14—15, the weak Christians had problems over diets and holy days, but it was the same basic issue.) There was a

potential division in the church, so the leaders asked Paul
for counsel.

Paul called to their attention three important factors.

(1) Knowledge (1 Cor. 8:1–2)

(2) Love (1 Cor. 8:3–6)

(3) Conscience (1 Cor. 8:7–13)

—*Be Wise*, pages 98–100

3. Review 1 Corinthians 8. What are the three main points Paul made in
this section? How do we temper knowledge with love, according to Paul?
Why is this important to the growth of the church?

## From the Commentary

There are dangers to maturity as well as to immaturity,
and one of them is overconfidence. When we think we are
strong, we discover that we are weak. The strong believer
who eats in the temple may find himself struggling with
an enemy who is too strong for him.

Paul did not suggest in 1 Corinthians 10:4 that an actual rock accompanied the Jews throughout their wilderness journey, though some Jewish rabbis taught this idea. It was a *spiritual* rock that supplied what they needed, and that Rock was Christ. Sometimes the water came from a rock (Ex. 17:1–7; Num. 20:7–11) and at other times from a well (Num. 21:16–18). God provided the water.

—*Be Wise*, page 102

4. What are the dangers to maturity? What are some of the ways overconfidence can lead to sin? According to Paul, how are we to deal with the temptation of overconfidence?

## From the Commentary

Paul issued a second warning: Good beginnings do not guarantee good endings (1 Cor. 10:5–12). The Jews experienced God's miracles, and yet they failed when they were tested in the wilderness. Experience must always be balanced with caution, for we never come to the place in our Christian walk where we are free from temptation and potential failure. All of the Jews twenty years old and upward who were rescued from Egypt, except for Joshua and Caleb, died in the wilderness during their years of wandering (Num. 14:26ff.).

We can hear some of the "strong" Corinthians asking, "But what does that have to do with us?" Paul then pointed out that the Corinthian church was guilty of the same sins that the Jews committed. Because of their lust for evil things, the Corinthians were guilty of immorality (1 Cor. 6), idolatry (1 Cor. 8; 10), and murmuring against God (2 Cor. 12:20–21). Like the nation of Israel, they were tempting God and just "daring Him" to act.

*—Be Wise*, page 102

5. Read Exodus 32; Numbers 11:4–34; and Numbers 21:4–6. How did Paul reference these passages in 1 Corinthians 10:1–12? What lessons did he draw from them that are relevant to the Corinthians? How are these lessons relevant to us?

## From the Commentary

Paul's third warning was that God can enable us to overcome temptation if we heed His Word (1 Cor. 10:13–22). God permits us to be tempted because He knows how much we can take; and He always provides a way to escape if we will trust Him and take advantage of it. The believer who thinks he can stand may fall; but the believer who flees will be able to stand.

Paul had already told his readers to "flee fornication" (1 Cor. 6:18); and now his warning is "Flee from idolatry" (1 Cor. 10:14). He explained the reason why: The idol itself is nothing, but it can be used by Satan to lead you into sin.

*—Be Wise*, page 103

6. Read Deuteronomy 32:17 and Psalm 106:37. What do these passages tell us about idolatry? Why is idolatry such a common theme in Paul's teaching? How is Paul's message in 1 Corinthians 10:13–22 similar to his teaching in 2 Corinthians 6:9–20?

## From the Commentary

At no time did Paul deny the freedom of the mature Christian to enjoy his privileges in Christ. "All things are lawful"—*but* not everything is profitable, and some things lead to slavery (1 Cor. 6:12). "All things are profitable"—*but* some activities can cause your weaker brother to stumble (1 Cor. 8:11–13). In other words, it is a mark of maturity when we balance our freedom with responsibility; otherwise, it ceases to be freedom and becomes anarchy, lawlessness.

To begin with, we have a responsibility to our fellow Christians in the church (1 Cor. 10:23–30). We are responsible to build others up in the faith and to seek their advantage. Philippians 2:1–4 gives the same admonition. While we do have freedom in Christ, we are not free to harm another believer.

—*Be Wise*, page 104

7. What are our privileges in Christ? What does it mean that all things are lawful but not all things are profitable? How did Paul caution the Corinthians regarding this liberty? What role does personal responsibility play in this?

## From the Commentary

> In the first half of 1 Corinthians 9, Paul proved that he
> had the right to receive financial support from the church
> at Corinth. He gave five arguments to support this
> contention.
>
> (1) His apostleship (vv. 1–6)
>
> (2) Human experience (v. 7)
>
> (3) The Old Testament law (vv. 8–12)
>
> (4) Old Testament practice (v. 13)
>
> (5) The teaching of Jesus (v. 14)
>
> —*Be Wise*, pages 112–14

8. Review Paul's arguments about his right to receive financial support
in 1 Corinthians 9:1–14. Why was it important for Paul to present
these arguments? What does this say about Paul? About the Corinthian
Christians? How do church leaders today defend their right to be supported
financially?

## From the Commentary

> Paul had the authority (right) to receive material support,
> but being a mature Christian, he balanced his authority
> with discipline. He did not have the right to give up
> his liberty in Christ, but he did have the liberty to give
> up his rights. Now we understand why he wrote as he
> did: He gave the Corinthian believers a living example
> of the very principles he was writing about. Should not
> the stronger believers in the church be able to set aside
> their rights for the sake of the weaker saints? Was eating
> meat more important than edifying the church?
>
> —*Be Wise*, page 115

9. Review 1 Corinthians 9:15–27. Why would Paul choose to give up his
rights? What message did he present in this passage? What does it teach us
about priorities for believers? How did Paul exemplify this?

*More to Consider: Read about Ananias and Sapphira (Acts 5:1–11)*
*and Simon the magician (Acts 8:18–24). What do these stories reveal*
*to us about the power of money to lead people into sin? How do stories*
*like these support Paul's discussion about money in 1 Corinthians?*

## From the Commentary

Paul was fond of athletic images and used them often
in his letters. The Corinthians would have been familiar
with the Greek Olympic Games as well as their own local
Isthmian Games. Knowing this, Paul used a metaphor
very close to their experience.

An athlete must be disciplined if he is to win the prize.
Discipline means giving up the good and the better for
the best. The athlete must watch his diet as well as his
hours. He must smile and say, "No, thank you," when
people offer him fattening desserts or invite him to late-
night parties. There is nothing wrong with food or fun,
but if they interfere with your highest goals, then they are
hindrances and not helps.

The Christian does not run the race in order to get to
heaven. He is in the race because he has been saved
through faith in Jesus Christ. Only Greek citizens were
allowed to participate in the games, and they had to obey
the rules both in their training and in their performing.
Any contestant found breaking the training rules was
automatically disqualified.

—*Be Wise*, pages 118–19

10. What did discipline look like to Paul? How do you balance authority with discipline? What is the price we have to pay to win the Lord's approval as believers? As leaders in ministry?

## Looking Inward

Take a moment to reflect on all that you've explored thus far in this study of 1 Corinthians 8—10. Review your notes and answers and think about how each of these things matters in your life today.

*Tips for Small Groups: To get the most out of this section, form pairs or trios and have group members take turns answering these questions. Be honest and as open as you can in this discussion, but most of all, be encouraging and supportive of others. Be sensitive to those who are going through particularly difficult times and don't press for people to speak if they're uncomfortable doing so.*

11. Have you ever been overconfident in your faith? What led to that? How did your overconfidence affect your ability to be faithful? What challenges did you face (or trigger) by your overconfidence? How can you temper this overconfidence with trust in God?

12. What does liberty mean for you? In what ways do you enjoy freedom in Christ? Do you decline to use some of the freedoms you have? If so, what are they and why do you choose to decline them?

13. What are some of the ways you practice discipline in your faith life? What are some areas where you could benefit from more discipline? How will you work on these?

## Going Forward

14. Think of one or two things that you have learned that you'd like to work on in the coming week. Remember that this is all about quality, not quantity. It's better to work on one specific area of life and do it well than to work on many and do poorly (or to be so overwhelmed that you simply don't try).

Do you need to be wiser in your use of liberty in Christ? Be specific. Go back through 1 Corinthians 8—10 and put a star next to the phrase or verse that is most encouraging to you. Consider memorizing this verse.

*Real-Life Application Ideas: Think about your liberty in Christ. What does that mean to you? What are examples in your life where you've chosen not to enjoy that liberty? Spend the next week looking for moments that represent your liberty and moments that reveal your responsibility with that liberty. Then reflect upon those moments and ask God for wisdom to help you know how to be responsible with the freedom He's given you. Do you need to act with more liberty or to restrain yourself in some area?*

## Seeking Help

15. Write a prayer below (or simply pray one in silence), inviting God to work on your mind and heart in those areas you've noted in the Going Forward section. Be honest about your desires and fears.

*Notes for Small Groups:*

- *Look for ways to put into practice the things you wrote in the Going Forward section. Talk with other group members about your ideas and commit to being accountable to one another.*

- *During the coming week, ask the Holy Spirit to continue to reveal truth to you from what you've read and studied.*

- *Before you start the next lesson, read 1 Corinthians 11—13. For more in-depth lesson preparation, read chapters 9 and 10, "Be Wise about Church Order" and "Be Wise about the Church Body," in* Be Wise.

# The Church Body
## (1 CORINTHIANS 11—13)

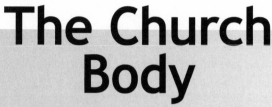

*Before you begin …*
- *Pray for the Holy Spirit to reveal truth and wisdom as you go through this lesson.*
- *Read 1 Corinthians 11—13. This lesson references chapters 9 and 10 in* Be Wise. *It will be helpful for you to have your Bible and a copy of the commentary available as you work through this lesson.*

## Getting Started

*From the Commentary*

The Christian faith brought freedom and hope to women, children, and slaves. It taught that all people, regardless of race or sex, were equal before their Creator, and that all believers were one in Jesus Christ (Gal. 3:28). As we have noted before, the local church was perhaps the only fellowship in the Roman Empire that welcomed all people, regardless of nationality, social status, sex, or economic position.

It was to be expected that there would be some who would carry this newfound freedom to excess. A new movement always suffers more from its disciples than from its enemies, and this was true in Corinth. Some of the women flaunted their "freedom" in the public meetings by refusing to cover their heads when they participated.

Paul did not forbid the women to pray or to prophesy. (Prophesying is not quite the same as our "preaching" or "expounding the Word." A person with the gift of prophecy proclaimed God's message as it was given to him *immediately* by the Spirit. The modern preacher studies the Word and prepares his message.) While the New Testament does not seem to permit women elders (1 Tim. 3:2), women in the early church who had the gift of prophecy were allowed to exercise it. They were also permitted to pray in the public meetings. However, they were not permitted to usurp authority over the men (1 Tim. 2:11–15) or to judge the messages of the other prophets (1 Cor. 14:27–35). If they had any questions, they were to ask their husbands (or other men) outside of the church meeting.

Eastern society at that time was very jealous over its women.

*—Be Wise*, page 124

1. Review 1 Corinthians 11:3–16. Respond to the statement "A new movement always suffers more from its disciples than its enemies." How

was this true in Paul's time, when Christianity was young? In what ways is this true today?

2. Choose one verse or phrase from 1 Corinthians 11—13 that stands out to you. This could be something you're intrigued by, something that makes you uncomfortable, something that puzzles you, something that resonates with you, or just something you want to examine further. Write that here.

## Going Deeper

*From the Commentary*

> There is a definite order of "headship" to the church: The Father is the Head over Christ, Christ is the Head of the man, and the man is the head of the woman. Some interpret *head* to mean "origin," but this would mean

that the Father originated Christ—something we cannot accept. In His redemptive ministry, the Son was subject to the Father even though He is equal to the Father (John 10:30; 14:28). Likewise, the woman is subject to the man even though to Christ she is equal to the man (1 Cor. 3:21–23; Gal. 3:28; Eph. 5:21–33).

Keep in mind that Paul was writing about the relationship *within the local assembly*, not in the world at large. It is God's plan that in the home and in the local church, the men should exercise headship under the authority of Jesus Christ.

—*Be Wise*, page 125

3. How much of what Paul taught about women in the church was specific to the culture of the time and how much is universally applicable even today? Why is this a controversial topic in today's church? What does headship mean today?

*More to Consider: Read John 12:1–3 and Luke 7:36–38, and notice what these women did with their hair. Given how significant a woman's hair was in Paul's culture, how would you expect people to interpret these women's actions?*

### From the Commentary

> Paul was arguing from the facts of creation, and the angels were a part of that creation. The angels also know their place and show respect when they worship God, for they cover their faces (Isa. 6:2). Finally, in some special way, the angels share in the public worship of the church and learn from the church (Eph. 3:10; 1 Peter 1:12). Public worship is a serious thing, for the angels are present; and we ought to conduct ourselves *as if we were in heaven.*
>
> —*Be Wise*, page 127

4. Why did Paul bring up angels in 1 Corinthians 11:10? What significance did angels have in Paul's time? How is that the same or different today? What does it mean to conduct ourselves in worship as if we are in heaven?

## From Today's World

The role of women in the church today varies dramatically from one denomination or group to another. While some continue to insist on men in leadership roles, others welcome women into some leadership roles, and others welcome them in any role, including that of lead pastor. This remains a contentious topic for some Christians, but it certainly has changed since the days of the early church, when women's roles were much less public.

5. Why does the role of women in the church remain a controversial topic? How does your church understand Paul's teaching on it? Should women be given the same leadership opportunities as men? Explain.

## From the Commentary

Since the beginning of the church, it was customary for the believers to eat together (Acts 2:42, 46). It was an opportunity for fellowship and for sharing with those who were less privileged. No doubt they climaxed this meal by observing the Lord's Supper. They called this meal "the love feast" since its main emphasis was showing love for the saints by sharing with one another.

The "agape feast" (from the Greek word for "love") was part of the worship at Corinth, but some serious abuses had crept in. As a result, the love feasts were doing more harm than good to the church. For one thing, there were various cliques in the church, and people ate with their own "crowd" instead of fellowshipping with the whole church family. While Paul condemned this selfish practice, he did take a positive view of the results: At least God would use this to reveal those who were true believers.

Another fault was selfishness: The rich people brought a great deal of food for themselves, while the poorer members went hungry. The original idea of the agape feast was sharing, but that idea had been lost.

—*Be Wise*, page 128

6. Review 1 Corinthians 11:17–22. What were the problems with the love feast? How are these similar to problems in today's church? Why do cliques form in churches? How can churches prevent that from happening? How can small groups avoid becoming harmful cliques?

## From the Commentary

Evangelical churches recognize two ordinances established by Jesus Christ for His people to observe: baptism and the Lord's Supper. (The Supper is also called *the Communion*, as in 1 Corinthians 10:16, and *the Eucharist*, which means "the giving of thanks.") Jesus Christ took the cup and the loaf—the ingredients of a common meal in that day—and transformed them into a meaningful spiritual experience for believers. However, the value of the experience depends on the condition of the hearts of those who participate; and this was the problem at Corinth.

It is a serious thing to come to the Communion with an unprepared heart. It is also a serious thing to receive the Supper in a careless manner. Because the Corinthians had been sinning in their observing of the Lord's Supper, God had disciplined them. "For this cause many are weak and sickly among you, and many sleep [have died]" (1 Cor. 11:30).

—*Be Wise*, page 129

7. Review 1 Corinthians 11:23–34. What does this passage tell us to do in order for the Lord's Supper to be a blessing and not a chastening? What attitude should we bring to the table? In what ways is the Lord's Supper an opportunity for spiritual growth?

*From the Commentary*

Since there was division in the Corinthian church, Paul began with an emphasis on the oneness of the church. He pointed out four wonderful bonds of spiritual unity. The first two are:

(1) We confess the same Lord (1 Cor. 12:1–3). Paul contrasted their experience as unconverted idolaters with their present experience as Christians. They had worshipped dead idols, but now they belonged to the living God. Their idols never spoke to them, but God spoke to them by His Spirit, and He even spoke *through* them in the gift of prophecy. When they were lost, they were under the control of the demons (1 Cor. 10:20) and were led astray ("carried away," 1 Cor. 12:2). But now the Spirit of God lived in them and directed them.

(2) We depend on the same God (1 Cor. 12:4–6). There is a trinitarian emphasis here: "the same Spirit … the same Lord … the same God." We individually may have different gifts, ministries, and ways of working, but "it is God which worketh in you both to will and to do of his good pleasure" (Phil. 2:13). The source of the gift is God; the sphere for administering the gift is from God; and the energy to use the gift is from God. Why, then, glorify men? Why compete with one another?

—*Be Wise*, pages 136–37

8. Review 1 Corinthians 12:1–13. Why was unity so important to the early church? Why is it important today? How unified are we in the modern church? How can Paul's teaching on the bonds of spiritual unity help the church become more unified today?

*More to Consider: Read Ephesians 4:3 and Matthew 24:14. What do these verses say about Christian unity? What is the purpose of Christian unity?*

## From the Commentary

The second two bonds of spiritual unity are:

(3) We minister to the same body (1 Cor. 12:7–11). The gifts are given for the good of the whole church. They are not for individual enjoyment, but for corporate employment. The Corinthians especially needed this reminder, because they were using their spiritual gifts selfishly to promote themselves and not to prosper the church. When we accept our gifts with humility, then we use them to promote harmony, and this helps the whole church.

(4) We have experienced the same baptism (1 Cor. 12:12–13). It is unfortunate that the term "baptism of the Spirit" has been divorced from its original New Testament meaning. God has spoken to us in Spirit-given *words* that we must not confuse (1 Cor. 2:12–13). The baptism of the Spirit occurs at conversion when the Spirit enters the believing sinner, gives him new life, and makes his body the temple of God. *All* believers have experienced this once-for-all baptism (1 Cor. 12:13). Nowhere does the Scripture command us to *seek* this baptism, because we have already experienced it and it need not be repeated.

—*Be Wise*, pages 137, 139

9. Why are the second reasons for unity (ministering to the same body, experiencing the same baptism) important to the church? How does the "baptism of the Spirit" unify? How can it divide? Why are the things Paul taught about regarding unity also the source of much division today?

## From the Commentary

Unity without diversity would produce uniformity, and uniformity tends to produce death. Life is a balance between unity and diversity. As a human body weakens, its systems slow down and everything tends to become uniform. The ultimate, of course, is that the body itself turns to dust.

This helps to explain why some churches (and other Christian ministries) have weakened and died: There was not sufficient diversity to keep unity from becoming uniformity. Dr. Vance Havner has expressed it: "First there is a man, then a movement, then a machine, and then a monument." Many ministries that began as a protest against "dead orthodoxy" became dead themselves, because in their desire to remain pure and doctrinally sound, they stifled creativity and new ideas.

—*Be Wise*, page 140

10. Review 1 Corinthians 12:14–31. How does diversity within the church help to maintain unity? When does diversity pose a challenge to unity? How can local churches foster both diversity and unity?

# Looking Inward

Take a moment to reflect on all that you've explored thus far in this study of 1 Corinthians 11—13. Review your notes and answers and think about how each of these things matters in your life today.

*Tips for Small Groups: To get the most out of this section, form pairs or trios and have group members take turns answering these questions. Be honest and as open as you can in this discussion, but most of all, be encouraging and supportive of others. Be sensitive to those who are going through particularly difficult times and don't press for people to speak if they're uncomfortable doing so.*

11. What are your thoughts about women having leadership positions in the church? Does your church encourage or discourage this? Explain. How do you think Paul's teaching on women should be applied today?

12. What are some ways you promote unity in your church? What are some things you do that might promote dissension instead? How unified is your church? What are the areas where your church can improve when it comes to unity?

13. Diversity is important to a church's character. What are some of the ways your church expresses its diversity? How does this diversity help your church in ministry? What are some ways you stand out as unique in your church? How can that contribute to the church's overall purpose?

## Going Forward

14. Think of one or two things that you have learned that you'd like to work on in the coming week. Remember that this is all about quality, not quantity. It's better to work on one specific area of life and do it well than to work on many and do poorly (or to be so overwhelmed that you simply don't try).

Do you want to contribute to unity in your church? Be specific. Go back through 1 Corinthians 11—13 and put a star next to the phrase or verse that is most encouraging to you. Consider memorizing this verse.

*Real-Life Application Ideas: Unity was Paul's big theme in 1 Corinthians 12. What are some practical ways you can promote unity in your small group? In your church? In your community? Come up with a few ideas for each, then do what it takes to implement these ideas. Keep in mind Paul's encouragements as well as his warnings.*

## Seeking Help

15. Write a prayer below (or simply pray one in silence), inviting God to work on your mind and heart in those areas you've noted in the Going Forward section. Be honest about your desires and fears.

*Notes for Small Groups:*

- *Look for ways to put into practice the things you wrote in the Going Forward section. Talk with other group members about your ideas and commit to being accountable to one another.*

- *During the coming week, ask the Holy Spirit to continue to reveal truth to you from what you've read and studied.*

- *Before you start the next lesson, read 1 Corinthians 14. For more in-depth lesson preparation, read chapter 11, "Be Wise about Using Spiritual Gifts," in* Be Wise.

# Spiritual Gifts
## (I CORINTHIANS 14)

*Before you begin ...*
- *Pray for the Holy Spirit to reveal truth and wisdom as you go through this lesson.*
- *Read 1 Corinthians 14. This lesson references chapter 11 in* Be Wise. *It will be helpful for you to have your Bible and a copy of the commentary available as you work through this lesson.*

## Getting Started

*From the Commentary*

Paul had discussed the gift of the Spirit, the gifts of the Spirit, and the graces of the Spirit; and now he concluded this section by explaining the government of the Spirit in the public worship services of the church. Apparently there was a tendency for some of the Corinthians to lose control of themselves as they exercised their gifts, and Paul had to remind them of the fundamental principles that ought to govern the public meetings of the church.

—*Be Wise*, page 149

1. Why is the "governing of the Spirit" important to the church? Why can't the different gifts be expressed however and whenever people want? What is the purpose of the guidelines Paul outlined in 1 Corinthians 14?

2. Choose one verse or phrase from 1 Corinthians 14 that stands out to you. This could be something you're intrigued by, something that makes you uncomfortable, something that puzzles you, something that resonates with you, or just something you want to examine further. Write that here.

# Going Deeper

*From the Commentary*

> *To edify* means "to build up." This concept is not alien
> to the "body" image of the church; even today, we speak
> about "bodybuilding exercises." There is an overlapping
> of images here, for the body of Christ is also the temple
> of the living God. Paul's choice of the word *edify* was a
> wise one.
>
> The mistake the Corinthians were making was to empha-
> size their own personal edification to the neglect of the
> church. They wanted to build themselves up, but they did
> not want to build up their fellow believers. This attitude,
> of course, not only hurt the other Christians, but it also
> hurt the believers who were practicing it. After all, if we
> are all members of the same body, the way we relate to
> the other members must ultimately affect us personally.
> "The eye cannot say unto the hand, I have no need of
> thee" (1 Cor. 12:21). If one member of the body is weak
> or infected, it will affect the other members.
>
> —*Be Wise*, pages 149–50

3. Review 1 Corinthians 14:1–5, 26. What did edification mean to the
early church? Why is this important today? How can people build one
another up in the church?

*More to Consider: Read Acts 2:1–13. What additional insight does this passage give us about the "tongues" Paul referred to in 1 Corinthians 14? How does this line up with Paul's teaching?*

## From the Commentary

Prophecy edifies the church, tongues edify only the speaker (1 Cor. 14:4–5). Paul did not deny the value of tongues to the speaker, but he did place a greater value on building up the church. "Greater is he that prophesieth than he that speaketh with tongues" (1 Cor. 14:5). Unless the tongues are interpreted (1 Cor. 12:10, 30), the message can do the church no good. Paul pointed out that an interpreter must be present before the gift of tongues may be exercised (1 Cor. 14:28).

Keep in mind that the members of the Corinthian church did not sit in the services with Bibles on their laps. The New Testament was being written, and the Old Testament scrolls were expensive and not available to most believers. God spoke to His people directly through the prophets, and the message was sometimes given in a tongue. The three gifts of knowledge, prophecy, and tongues worked together to convey truth to the people (1 Cor. 13:1–2, 8–11).

—*Be Wise*, page 151

4. What is Paul's emphasis in 1 Corinthians 14? What happens to doctrinal teaching when it's not based on God's truth? How were the Corinthians struggling with this?

## From Today's World

Spiritual gifts and how they're interpreted constitute some of the more obvious distinguishing characteristics of different denominations and churches around the world. Where one church emphasizes the gift of speaking in tongues, another might downplay it to the point of irrelevance. When there is disagreement *within* a church body on the gifts (a surprisingly frequent occurrence), a church is at risk for a split. People are passionate about their interpretations of 1 Corinthians 14 (and other passages on spiritual gifts). Paul's dream of unity is often put to the test when it comes to spiritual gifts.

5. Why is this topic so contentious for Christians? Which spiritual gifts cause the most dissension in churches? What are some ways a church can overcome this disagreement? Is it possible for a church to be all things to all people when it comes to spiritual gifts? Explain.

*From the Commentary*

> Eight times in 1 Corinthians 14:6–25, Paul used the
> word *understanding*. It is not enough for the minister to
> impart information to people; the people must *receive* it if
> it is to do them any good. The seed that is received in the
> good ground is the seed that bears fruit, but this means
> that there must be an *understanding* of the Word of God
> (Matt. 13:23). If a believer wants to be edified, he must
> prepare his heart to receive the Word (1 Thess. 2:13). Not
> everybody who *listens* really *hears*.
>
> —*Be Wise*, page 152

6. Circle the use of the word *understanding* in 1 Corinthians 14:6–25.
(Your translation may have *intelligible, mind, thinking*, etc.) Why was
understanding such an important message for Paul? How do believers
prepare their hearts to receive God's Word?

*From the Commentary*

> First Corinthians 14:10 gives us good reason to believe
> that, when Paul wrote about tongues, he was referring
> to known languages and not some "heavenly" language.
> Each language is different and yet each language has its
> own meaning. No matter how sincere a speaker may be,
> if I do not understand his language, he cannot communi-
> cate with me. To the Greeks, a *barbarian* was the lowest
> person on the social or national ladder. In fact, anybody
> who was not a Greek was considered a barbarian.
>
> —*Be Wise*, page 153

7. What is it about 1 Corinthians 14:10 that suggests the languages are
known? Why would this have been significant to the Corinthian church?
To today's church? How might this affect the way some churches worship
today?

## From the Commentary

As a nation, the Jews were always seeking a sign (Matt. 12:38; 1 Cor. 1:22). At Pentecost, the fact that the apostles spoke in tongues was a sign to the unbelieving Jews who were there celebrating the feast. The miracle of tongues aroused their interest, but it did not convict their hearts. It took Peter's preaching (in Aramaic, which the people all understood) to bring them to the place of conviction and conversion.

The principle of *edification* encourages us to major on sharing the Word of God so that the church will be strengthened and grow. The principle of *understanding* reminds us that what we share must be understood if it is to do any good. The private use of spiritual gifts may edify the user, but it will not edify the church; and Paul admonished us to "excel to the edifying of the church" (1 Cor. 14:12).

—*Be Wise*, page 155

8. What is it about speaking in tongues that edifies? Can this be a gift that edifies the body? How, or why not? How can other spiritual gifts be wrongly used to edify the user only? What are the dangers of mistaking private edification for public?

## From the Commentary

The Corinthian church was having special problems with disorder in their public meetings (1 Cor. 11:17–23). The reason is not difficult to determine: They were using their spiritual gifts to please themselves and not to help their brethren. The key word was not *edification*, but *exhibition*. If you think that *your* contribution to the service is more important than your brother's contribution, then you will either be impatient until he finishes, or you will interrupt him. Add to this problem the difficulties caused by the "liberated women" in the assembly, and you can understand why the church experienced carnal confusion.

—*Be Wise*, page 156

9. Read 1 Corinthians 14:26. In what ways is this a snapshot of worship in the early church? What roles did people have in this worship? How might we use this as a model for worship today? Is it necessary or helpful to do that?

## From the Commentary

Paul summarized the main teachings of 1 Corinthians 14 in verses 39–40. Prophecy is more important than tongues, but the church should not prohibit the correct exercise of the gift of tongues. The purpose of spiritual gifts is the edification of the whole church, and therefore, gifts must be exercised in an orderly manner. Public worship must be carried on "in a seemly manner," that is, with beauty, order, and spiritual motivation and content.

Before leaving this chapter, it might be helpful to summarize what Paul wrote about the gift of tongues. It is the God-given ability to speak in a known language with which the speaker was not previously acquainted. The purpose was not to win the lost, but to edify the saved. Not every believer had this gift, nor was this gift an evidence of spirituality or the result of a "baptism of the Spirit."

Only three persons were permitted to speak in tongues in any one meeting, and they had to do so in order and with interpretation. If there was no interpreter, they had to keep silent. Prophecy is the superior gift, but tongues were not to be despised if they were exercised according to Scripture.

When the foundational work of the apostles and prophets ended, it would seem that the gifts of knowledge, prophecy, and tongues would no longer be needed. "Whether there be tongues, they shall cease" (1 Cor. 13:8). Certainly

God could give this gift today if He pleased, but I am not prepared to believe that every instance of tongues is divinely energized. Nor would I go so far as to say that all instances of tongues are either satanic or self-induced.

It is unfortunate when believers make tongues a test of fellowship or spirituality. That in itself would alert me that the Spirit would not be at work. Let's keep our priorities straight and major on winning the lost and building the church.

—*Be Wise*, page 160

10. In 1 Corinthians 14, Paul offered specific guidelines for the gift of tongues. What does this reveal about the early church? What wisdom can it provide for resolving dissension in today's church? How can Paul's teaching help to unite church bodies that are split on this topic?

## Looking Inward

Take a moment to reflect on all that you've explored thus far in this study of 1 Corinthians 14. Review your notes and answers and think about how each of these things matters in your life today.

*Tips for Small Groups: To get the most out of this section, form pairs or trios and have group members take turns answering these questions. Be honest and as open as you can in this discussion, but most of all, be encouraging and supportive of others. Be sensitive to those who are going through particularly difficult times and don't press for people to speak if they're uncomfortable doing so.*

11. How well do you understand the gifts of the Spirit? Which gifts do you feel you have? How do those gifts manifest themselves? What are some things you wish you understood about the spiritual gifts?

12. What are some examples of personal or private edification you've enjoyed from the use of spiritual gifts? What are some public examples? How do you know if you're using your gifts for the greater good?

13. What is your experience with the gift of tongues? Has it encouraged you? Caused you discomfort? What is your opinion on its place in the church? How can people who embrace this gift maintain unity with those who don't?

## Going Forward

14. Think of one or two things that you have learned that you'd like to work on in the coming week. Remember that this is all about quality, not quantity. It's better to work on one specific area of life and do it well than to work on many and do poorly (or to be so overwhelmed that you simply don't try).

Do you want to better use the different gifts of the Spirit for the good of the body of Christ? Be specific. Go back through 1 Corinthians 14 and put a star next to the phrase or verse that is most encouraging to you. Consider memorizing this verse.

> *Real-Life Application Ideas: There are many spiritual-gift inventories available in the marketplace, and one of those could help you identify what your gifts are. Alternatively, you could pray and think about these questions: How has God worked through me? Are there any patterns in the way God works through me? If you have already discovered your strengths in the area of service, how might God want to work through you to utilize those strengths for His glory? You can also ask other Christians who know you well how they think you have served or could serve well. Remember that no area of service is more glamorous in God's eyes than another.*

## Seeking Help

15. Write a prayer below (or simply pray one in silence), inviting God to work on your mind and heart in those areas you've noted in the Going Forward section. Be honest about your desires and fears.

*Notes for Small Groups:*

- *Look for ways to put into practice the things you wrote in the Going Forward section. Talk with other group members about your ideas and commit to being accountable to one another.*

- *During the coming week, ask the Holy Spirit to continue to reveal truth to you from what you've read and studied.*

- *Before you start the next lesson, read 1 Corinthians 15—16. For more in-depth lesson preparation, read chapters 12 and 13, "Be Wise about the Resurrection" and "Be Wise about Christian Stewardship," in* Be Wise.

# The Resurrection
## (1 CORINTHIANS 15—16)

*Before you begin …*
- *Pray for the Holy Spirit to reveal truth and wisdom as you go through this lesson.*
- *Read 1 Corinthians 15—16. This lesson references chapters 12 and 13 in* Be Wise. *It will be helpful for you to have your Bible and a copy of the commentary available as you work through this lesson.*

## Getting Started

### From the Commentary

It is important to note that the believers at Corinth did believe in the resurrection of Jesus Christ; so Paul started his argument with that fundamental truth. He presented three proofs to assure his readers that Jesus Christ indeed had been raised from the dead.

Proof #1—their salvation (1 Cor. 15:1–2). Paul had come to Corinth and preached the message of the gospel, and their faith had transformed their lives. But an integral part of the gospel message was the fact of Christ's resurrection. After all, a dead Savior cannot save anybody.

Proof #2—the Old Testament Scriptures (1 Cor. 15:3–4). *First of all* means "of first importance." The gospel is the most important message that the church ever proclaims. While it is good to be involved in social action and the betterment of mankind, there is no reason why these ministries should preempt the gospel. "Christ died ... he was buried ... he rose again ... he was seen" are the basic historical *facts* on which the gospel stands (1 Cor. 15:3–5). "Christ died *for our sins*" is the theological explanation of the historical facts.

When Paul wrote "according to the scriptures" (1 Cor. 15:3) he was referring to the Old Testament Scriptures. Much of the sacrificial system in the Old Testament pointed to the sacrifice of Christ as our substitute and Savior. The annual Day of Atonement (Lev. 16) and prophecies like Isaiah 53 would also come to mind.

Proof #3—Christ was seen by witnesses (1 Cor. 15:5–11). On the cross, Jesus was exposed to the eyes of unbelievers; but after the resurrection, He was seen by believers who could be witnesses of His resurrection (Acts 1:22; 2:32; 3:15; 5:32). Peter saw Him and so did the disciples collectively. James was a half brother of the Lord who became a believer after the Lord appeared to him (John 7:5; Acts 1:14). The five hundred *plus* brethren all saw Him at the same time (1 Cor. 15:6), so it could not have been a hallucination or a deception. This event may have been just before His ascension (Matt. 28:16ff.).

—*Be Wise*, pages 163–65

1. Review 1 Corinthians 15:1–19. Why did the Corinthian church need to be reassured about Jesus' resurrection with Paul's proofs? Why might they have been suffering from doubt? How can these same proofs encourage the church today?

*More to Consider: Paul made it clear that his salvation was purely an act of God's grace; but that grace worked in and through him as he served the Lord. Read Zechariah 12:10—13:6 and 1 Timothy 1:16. How might these verses explain Paul's mention of being "abnormally born" (1 Cor. 15:8)?*

2. Choose one verse or phrase from 1 Corinthians 15—16 that stands out to you. This could be something you're intrigued by, something that makes you uncomfortable, something that puzzles you, something that resonates with you, or just something you want to examine further. Write that here.

# Going Deeper

*From the Commentary*

Paul used three images to answer the question "When are the dead raised?"

(1) Firstfruits (1 Cor. 15:20, 23). We have already noted this reference to the Old Testament feast (Lev. 23:9–14). As the Lamb of God, Jesus died on Passover. As the sheaf of firstfruits, He arose from the dead three days later on the first day of the week. When the priest waved the sheaf of the firstfruits before the Lord, it was a sign that the entire harvest belonged to Him. When Jesus was raised from the dead, it was God's assurance to us that we shall also be raised one day as part of that future harvest. To believers, death is only "sleep." The body sleeps, but the soul is at home with the Lord (2 Cor. 5:1–8; Phil. 1:21–23). At the resurrection, the body will be "awakened" and glorified.

(2) Adam (1 Cor. 15:21–22). Paul saw in Adam a type of Jesus Christ *by the way of contrast* (see also Rom. 5:12–21). The first Adam was made from the earth, but the Last Adam (Christ, 1 Cor. 15:45–47) came from heaven. The first Adam disobeyed God and brought sin and death into the world, but the Last Adam obeyed the Father and brought righteousness and life.

(3) The kingdom (1 Cor. 15:24–28). When Jesus Christ comes to the earth to judge, He will banish sin for a thousand years and establish His kingdom (Rev.

20:1–6). Believers will reign with Him and share His glory and authority. This kingdom, prophesied in the Old Testament, is called "the millennium" by prophetic teachers. The word comes from the Latin: *mille*— thousand, *annum*—year.

—*Be Wise*, pages 166–67

3. Why would the Corinthians have been concerned about when they would be resurrected? What sorts of persecution might they have been enduring? What was Paul's main purpose in answering this question? How can the modern church benefit from Paul's answer?

## From the Commentary

The resurrection of the human body is a future event that has compelling implications for our personal lives. If the resurrection is not true, then we can forget about the future and live as we please! But the resurrection *is* true! Jesus *is* coming again! Even if we die before He comes, we shall be raised at His coming and stand before Him in a glorified body.

—*Be Wise*, page 167

4. Review 1 Corinthians 15:29–34, 49–58. What do these verses reveal about why believers are resurrected? How might this have been a comfort to the early church? How is it a comfort for us today?

## From the Commentary

> When Paul said "I die daily," he was not referring to "dying to self," as in Romans 6, but to the physical dangers he faced as a servant of Christ (2 Cor. 4:8—5:10; 11:23–28). He was in constant jeopardy from his enemies and on more than one occasion had been close to death. Why endure suffering and danger if death ends it all? "Let us eat and drink; for tomorrow we shall die" (Isa. 22:13).
>
> What we do in the body in this life comes up for review at the judgment seat of Christ (2 Cor. 5:10). God deals with the *whole* person, not just with the "soul."
>
> —*Be Wise*, page 168

5. Why is the future resurrection important for those who are suffering in body today? What are some of the ways Christians today are suffering? How

can the promise of the resurrection help them through these challenging times?

## From the Commentary

> Sin, death, and the law go together. The law reveals sin, and the "wages of sin is death" (Rom. 6:23). Jesus bore our sins on the cross (1 Peter 2:24), and also bore the curse of the law (Gal. 3:13). It is through Him that we have this victory, and we share the victory *today*. The literal translation of 1 Corinthians 15:57 is, "But thanks be to God who *keeps on giving us the victory* through our Lord Jesus Christ." We experience "the power of his resurrection" in our lives as we yield to Him (Phil. 3:10).
>
> —*Be Wise*, page 169

6. In what ways is 1 Corinthians 15:57 a hymn of praise? What is the admonition to the church in this verse? How is this verse an answer to the cry that "everything is meaningless" (Eccl. 1:2)?

## From the Commentary

> Being philosophers, the Greeks reasoned that the resur-
> rection of the human body was an impossibility. After all,
> when the body turned to dust, it became soil from which
> other bodies derived nourishment. In short, the food that
> we eat is a part of the elements of the bodies of genera-
> tions long gone. When the body of the founder of Rhode
> Island, Roger Williams, was disinterred, it was discovered
> that the roots of a nearby apple tree had grown through
> the coffin. To some degree, the people who ate the apples
> partook of his body. At the resurrection, then, who will
> claim the various elements?
>
> —*Be Wise*, page 170

7. Review 1 Corinthians 15:35–48. What was Paul's response to the reasoning that the resurrection was impossible? How did Paul's answer satisfy the question while also acknowledging the mystery of the resurrection?

*More to Consider: What do the following passages teach us about hell: Matthew 25:41; 2 Thessalonians 1:7–10; and Revelation 20:11–15? What should such knowledge inspire us to do?*

## From the Commentary

One of the most important ministries Paul had during his third journey was the gathering of a special "relief offering" for the poor believers in Jerusalem. He wanted to achieve several purposes in this offering. For one thing, the Gentiles owed material help to the Jews in return for the spiritual blessings the Jews had given them (Rom. 15:25–27). At the Jerusalem Conference years before, Paul had agreed to "remember the poor," so he was keeping his pledge (Gal. 2:10). Paul not only preached the gospel, but he also tried to assist those who had physical and material needs.

Why was there such a great need in the Jerusalem church? It is likely that many of the believers had been visiting Jerusalem at Pentecost when they heard the Word and were saved. This meant that they were strangers, without employment, and the church would have to care for them. In the early days of the church, the members had gladly shared with each other (Acts 2:41–47; 4:33–37); but even their resources were limited. There had also been a famine (Acts 11:27–30), and the relief sent at that time could not last for too long a time.

—*Be Wise*, pages 175–76

8. What does 1 Corinthians 16:1–4 teach us about giving? About the importance of meeting the needs of our brothers and sisters in Christ? What does it teach us about responding to greater times of need in the world?

## From the Commentary

Paul informed his friends at Corinth of his plans for future travel and ministry. It is worth noting that his statements were very tentative: "It may be suitable … it may be … wherever I go … but I trust." Of course, the entire plan was dependent on God's providential leading: "if the Lord permit." Paul's attitude toward his future plans agreed with the injunctions in James 4:13–17.

Paul was at Ephesus when he wrote this letter. His plan was to travel to Macedonia for a time of ministry (*pass through* in 1 Corinthians 16:5 means "travel in a systematic ministry"), winter at Corinth, and then go to Judea with the collection. From November to February, it was impossible to travel by ship; so it would have been convenient for Paul to stay at Corinth and be with his friends. There were some problems to solve in the church, and Paul had promised to come to help the leaders (1 Cor. 11:34).

—*Be Wise*, pages 178–79

9. What does Paul's plan (or hoped-for plan) tell us about his love for the Corinthian church? What lessons can we glean from this simple section of Scripture where Paul promised to visit again (1 Cor. 16:5–9)? How can we embrace a similar attitude of courage and commitment to help our fellow believers? What would that look like in the local church?

## From the Commentary

Often at the close of his letters, Paul named various people who were a part of his life and his ministry; and what a variety they were! He was not only a soul winner, but he was a friend maker; and many of his friends found their way into dedicated service for the Lord. Evangelist Dwight L. Moody possessed this same gift of making friends and then enlisting them for the Lord's service. Some of the greatest preachers and musicians of the late nineteenth and early twentieth centuries were "found" by Moody, including Ira Sankey, G. Campbell Morgan, Henry Drummond, and F. B. Meyer.

Money and opportunities are valueless without people. The church's greatest asset is people, and yet too often the church takes people for granted. Jesus did not give His disciples money, but He did invest three years training them for service so they might seize the opportunities He would present them. If *people* are prepared, then God will supply both the *opportunities* and the *money* so that His work will be accomplished.

—*Be Wise*, page 181

10. What is notable about Paul's closing at the end of 1 Corinthians (16:10–24)? How did he use encouragement in these verses? Why is it significant that he noted he wrote "in his own hand"? (Most letters were dictated to a scribe at the time.)

## Looking Inward

Take a moment to reflect on all that you've explored thus far in this study of 1 Corinthians 15—16. Review your notes and answers and think about how each of these things matters in your life today.

*Tips for Small Groups: To get the most out of this section, form pairs or trios and have group members take turns answering these questions. Be honest and as open as you can in this discussion, but most of all, be encouraging and supportive of others. Be sensitive to those who are going through particularly difficult times and don't press for people to speak if they're uncomfortable doing so.*

11. Have you ever had doubts about Jesus' resurrection? What led to those doubts? How have you worked through them? Why is it important to you that Jesus rose from the dead? Are you more like Thomas (a doubter) or Mary (who was quick to believe)?

12. In what ways do you live in anticipation of your own resurrection? Do you think about life after death much? Why or why not? How has the promise of resurrection helped you through difficult times? How does the

promise and hope of resurrection affect the manner in which you live out your faith?

13. Paul was a great encourager, even after speaking directly to issues that were difficult in a local church. What are some ways you encourage the people in your life? What are some ways they encourage you? What are some things you can do to encourage others more?

## Going Forward

14. Think of one or two things that you have learned that you'd like to work on in the coming week. Remember that this is all about quality, not quantity. It's better to work on one specific area of life and do it well than to work on many and do poorly (or to be so overwhelmed that you simply don't try).

Do you want to live in light of the resurrection of believers? Be specific. Go back through 1 Corinthians 15—16 and put a star next to the phrase or verse that is most encouraging to you. Consider memorizing this verse.

*Real-Life Application Ideas: Paul's teaching always ends with kind and inspirational words to those reading the letter. Take a few minutes to write some encouraging letters to people in your life. Be sincere and specific in your encouragement.*

## Seeking Help

15. Write a prayer below (or simply pray one in silence), inviting God to work on your mind and heart in those areas you've noted in the Going Forward section. Be honest about your desires and fears.

*Notes for Small Groups:*

- *Look for ways to put into practice the things you wrote in the Going Forward section. Talk with other group members about your ideas and commit to being accountable to one another.*

- *During the coming week, ask the Holy Spirit to continue to reveal truth to you from what you've read and studied.*

# Summary and Review

*Notes for Small Groups: This session is a summary and review of this book. Because of that, it is shorter than the previous lessons. If you are using this in a small-group setting, consider combining this lesson with a time of fellowship or a shared meal.*

*Before you begin ...*
- *Pray for the Holy Spirit to reveal truth and wisdom as you go through this lesson.*
- *Briefly review the notes you made in the previous sessions. You will refer back to previous sections throughout this bonus lesson.*

## Looking Back

1. Over the past eight lessons, you've examined many challenging and inspiring messages in Paul's first letter to the Corinthians. What expectations did you bring to this study? In what ways were those expectations met?

2. What is the most significant personal discovery you've made from this study?

3. What surprised you most about Paul's emphasis on unity? What, if anything, troubled you?

## Progress Report

4. Take a few moments to review the Going Forward sections of the previous lessons. How would you rate your progress for each of the things you chose to work on? What adjustments, if any, do you need to make to continue on the path toward spiritual maturity?

5. In what ways have you grown closer to Christ during this study? Take a moment to celebrate those things. Then think of areas where you feel you still need to grow and note those here. Make plans to revisit this study in a few weeks to review your growing faith.

## Things to Pray About

6. First Corinthians is a book about wisdom, confronting sin, and building unity in the church. As you reflect on these themes, consider how they apply to you individually, and also to your church body.

7. The messages in 1 Corinthians include dealing with sexual impurity, marriage and divorce, liberty, and the importance of Jesus' resurrection. Spend time praying for each of these topics.

8. Whether you've been studying this in a small group or on your own, there are many other Christians working through the very same issues you discovered when examining 1 Corinthians. Take time to pray for them, that God would reveal truth, that the Holy Spirit would guide you, and that each person might grow in spiritual maturity according to God's will.

## A Blessing of Encouragement

Studying the Bible is one of the best ways to learn how to be more like Christ. Thanks for taking this step. In closing, let this blessing precede you and follow you into the next week while you continue to marinate in God's Word:

*May God light your path to greater understanding as you review the truths found in 1 Corinthians and consider how they can help you grow closer to Christ.*